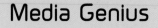

Media Genius

CREATE YOUR OWN

MOVIE OR TV SHOW

Matt Anniss

CAPSTONE PRESS
a Capstone imprint

© 2017 Heinemann-Raintree
an imprint of Capstone Global Library, LLC
Chicago, Illinois

To contact Capstone Global Library please call 800-747-4992, or visit our web site
www.capstonepub.com

Edited by James Benefield and Helen Cox Cannons
Designed by Steve Mead
Original illustrations © Capstone Global Library Ltd 2016
Picture research by Morgan Walters
Production by Victoria Fitzgerald
Originated by Capstone Global Library Ltd
Printed and bound in China

20 19 18 17 16
10 9 8 7 6 5 4 3 2 1

Library of Congress Cataloging-in-Publication Data
Cataloging-in-publication data is available at the Library of Congress.
ISBN 978-1-4109-8110-3 (hardback)
ISBN 978-1-4109-8114-1 (ebook PDF)

Acknowledgments
The author and publisher are grateful to the following for permission to reproduce copyright
material: Alamy: Image Source Plus, 12; Corbis: 2/Ocean, cover, 42, Frederic Soltan, 36, Louie
Psihoyos, 35, TWPhoto, 30; Getty Images: Hill Street Studios, 18, James Devaney, 43, Leon
Bennett, 17, Matt Carr, 41, Matthew Horwood, 10, Peter Bischoff, 4, Pool APESTEGUY/
SIMON, 31, Rachel Murray, 5, Syfy, 21, Thinkstock Images, 23; iStockphoto:lovleah, 26, Pamela
Moore, 39; Newscom: Dave Penman/REX, 9; Shutterstock: Alexandru Nika, 7, Alexey Boldin,
(phone) top 25, ChameleonsEye, 20, Christian Bertrand, 29, cobalt88, (TV) 8, (tablet) middle
25, Denis Dryashkin, 37, Goodluz, 40, Gorosi, 6, keellla, (video camera) bottom 25, Kzenon,
28, Margarita Vodopyanova, 24, MaxyM, 19, Monkey Business Images, 32, Nenov Brothers
Images, (webcam) middle 25, PAN Photo Agency, 38, Rashevskyi Viacheslav, bottom 13, Salim
October, (reporter) 8, Samo Trebizan, 34, Samuel Borges Photography, top 13, Sergey Novikov,
33, Syda Productions, 16, Tom Wang, 22, Zurijeta, 14

We would like to thank Nicola Armitage for her invaluable help in the preparation of this book.

PO007590LEOF16

Table of Contents

Do It Yourself!

Do you dream of being the next Steven Spielberg? Do you have a desire to make people laugh, cry, or think deeply? Or perhaps you'd like to tell a great story, or present surprising or little-known facts in an entertaining way? If your answer is "yes" to any of those questions, you may want to consider making your own movies and TV shows! It would have once been beyond the means of most young people to make a movie or TV program. Filmmaking is now accessible to almost anyone, thanks to modern technology.

Lots of people, money, and equipment are needed to make Hollywood blockbusters. However, you can also get great results with just a few friends and your smartphone!

Between 2009 and 2014, six American teenagers ran their own TV channel on YouTube called Our2ndLife. It turned them into worldwide stars, with nearly 3 million people tuning in to watch their weekly video updates. One member of the group, Trevor Moran, posted his first clip on YouTube when he was just 10 years old!

Quick and easy

Filmmaking is an easy hobby to start—you may already have some of the equipment available! For example, if you have access to a webcam, smartphone, digital camera, or tablet computer, then you're pretty much ready to start. Once you've read this book, you'll know just how easy it is to film something cool and edit it into an amazing video on your computer. You're then ready to share your work, if you want to.

Many filmmakers start out this way. Today, an increasing number of people working in the movie and TV industry got their big break after sharing home movies online. There are many web sites you can use to share things you film, but one of the most popular is YouTube.

CHAPTER 1

Choosing Your Style

It's useful to take some time to think about the style of movie or TV show you'd like to make. For example, you need to choose between fact and fiction.

Spend an afternoon flipping between TV channels and you'll see just how many different types of movies and shows you could make.

Separating fact from fiction

Factual movies and TV shows are about real things, people, places, and events. This is sometimes called nonfiction. Everything else is classified as fiction. Overall, fictional works are created purely for entertainment. Fiction contains stories, characters, and situations thought up by a writer.

Factual movies and shows can also be entertaining. However, the main reason factual shows and movies are created is to be informative. They might explain how animals live their lives, why historical events took place, or what's happening in the world.

Are you struggling to choose between these two styles of filmmaking? The following multiple-choice quiz could help.

FACT or FICTION?

Which of the following most appeals to you?
A: Learning new things
B: Writing stories

Which of the following do you most enjoy?
A: Meeting new people and hearing their stories
B: Making my friends laugh

Which of the following would you most like to film?
A: Interesting things happening in my neighborhood
B: People in costumes acting out stories

What would be your ideal role in a movie or TV show?
A: I'd like to film, direct, and interview people on camera
B: I'd like to direct and perform

If you answered mostly...
A: You're a born factual filmmaker
B: You should concentrate on fictional movies and TV shows

That's a fact!

Deciding between focusing on fact or fiction is merely the beginning of your filmmaking journey. Next, you need to decide on the style of movie or show you wish to make.

Different styles are sometimes called genres. Grouping movies and TV shows by their genres helps people know what to expect. Popular factual genres include:

CURRENT AFFAIRS

Current affairs programs focus on contemporary events. Content includes news reports and investigations into issues that affect our day-to-day lives. They're based on facts and include interviews with people close to the story.

DOCUMENTARIES

Documentaries explore an interesting subject in greater depth. Documentaries often use a combination of interviews and film footage. Some of the most popular ones focus on the natural world. A great example is *March of the Penguins*.

DOCU-DRAMA

Docu-dramas blur the boundaries between fact and fiction, by getting actors to re-create real events. Docu-dramas often focus on events from history or amazing real-life stories.

Television news is the world's most popular style of factual programming. However, there are many other options for would-be factual filmmakers.

Some of the most popular TV series are those that focus on the world around us, such as *Africa*, *Frozen Planet*, and *Secret Life of Birds*, all hosted by David Attenborough. However, filming animals in the wild can be difficult and dangerous, so it should only be done by trained professionals.

The long or short of it

Factual movies and programs can be as simple or complicated as you wish. For example, it wouldn't take you long to make a short news report about your school basketball team. However, filming a documentary about the history of basketball would take much longer.

Success Story

According to the Guinness World Records, the world's most popular factual TV series is *Top Gear*. This British show about cars has been shown in 212 different countries worldwide!

In fictional movie and TV genres, you can let your imagination run wild—just like the creators of *Doctor Who* do. There's almost no limit to the weird and wonderful things that you can come up with.

POLICE PUBLIC CALL BOX

POLICE TELEPHONE
FREE
FOR USE OF
PUBLIC
ADVICE & ASSIST...
OBTAINABLE IMME...
OFFICERS & C...
RESPOND TO ALL...
PULL TO...

Use your imagination!

If you had to list your favorite movies and TV programs, how many would be works of fiction? Unless you only watch documentaries and news programs, most of what you watch is probably going to be fiction. So what kind of fictional shows do you enjoy the most?

When it comes to fiction, there are many genres for budding filmmakers to choose from. Comedies make us laugh, and dramas tell gripping stories about believable characters in real-world situations. Also popular is science fiction (sometimes shortened to "sci-fi"), which is about possible future worlds.

Styles within styles

Many of these movie and TV genres have their own sub-genres. These are like styles within a style. Below are a few genres and some of the sub-genres associated with them. How many more can you think of?

DRAMA
Police show
Gangster movie
Medical drama
Soap opera
Thriller
Film noir

COMEDY
Stand-up comedy
Sketch comedy
Sitcom
Cartoon
Romantic comedy
Buddy movie

SCI-FI
Time travel
Superheroes
Space travel
Horror

ENTERTAINMENT
Game show
Talk show
Variety show
Reality television

No limits!

These genres, sub-genres, and formats are merely a guide. Many of the best movies and TV shows bend these rules, either by combining two or more styles or even creating a new sub-genre of their own. There's no limit to what you can do—let your imagination run free and see what you can come up with!

Start small or aim high?

When deciding whether to make a movie or a TV show, ask yourself this: Do you want to work alone, with a small group of friends, or involve lots of people? The more complicated and ambitious your project, the more help you'll need. For example, you could make a documentary TV program by yourself. You'll just need to do all the filming and interview all the people. Making stuff gets more complicated if you want to tell a story over the course of a movie or over several episodes of a TV series. You'll need people to act, take care of costumes, help you film, and more.

You might dream of making an epic movie, but starting with a short TV show on your own may be easier.

The way people watch movies and TV shows is changing. Many people now choose to watch their entertainment online. Every month, more than a billion people watch videos on YouTube, the world's most popular video-sharing web site. According to experts, videos stand a greater chance of attracting viewers if they're relatively short. The average length of the 100 most popular YouTube clips is just 5 minutes.

Money matters

Then there's the issue of cost. According to movie industry research, average production costs of a Hollywood movie in 2013 were an astonishing $71 million. Not all successful movies cost this much to make, of course. The 2004 movie *My Big Fat Greek Wedding* cost an estimated $5 million to make, but earned over $370 million in total worldwide.

Most filmmakers don't have piles of cash, however. And you can make fun movies and TV shows with little or no budget—just the cost of a smartphone and any editing technology that you may want to buy. You can save costs by borrowing equipment. You can also ask friends to film and act for free.

CHAPTER 2

Planning Your MOVIE or TV SHOW

Now you have an idea of the kind of movie or TV show you'd like to make. The next step is to figure out how you're going to make it. There are many things you'll need to think about, including:

- How long is the movie or TV show going to be?
- Will it be a one-time show or movie, or will it be split into several episodes?
- What equipment will I need and where will I film?
- Whom will it focus on?

You're probably eager to get that camera in your hands. However, before you get started, you will need to do some careful planning.

Figure it out

Figuring out a rough structure is a good place to start. How do you want your movie or TV show to begin and end? Once you know this, you can flesh out the story in between.

THE KNOWLEDGE

Many movies and TV shows use a blueprint known as the Three-Act Structure. Think of it as a line with a beginning, middle, and end. The first and final acts are usually of a similar length, with the middle act being a little longer.

Act 1
This introduces the characters and sets up the story. Toward the end of the act, there will be a plot point— a major twist in the story to keep viewers interested.

Act 2
This is the middle section of the movie or show. It usually includes a twist called the midpoint roughly halfway through. There is usually a second plot point at the end.

Act 3
This is the conclusion of the story, or climax. It wraps up the plot with the story's characters somehow changed.

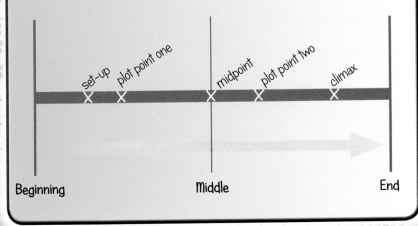

set-up plot point one midpoint plot point two climax

Beginning Middle End

Research and planning

The best factual movies and shows, particularly documentaries, have two key elements:

WELL-RESEARCHED FACTS

These can be taken from books, newspapers, TV news reports, and web sites. Some sources are more reliable than others. For example, an article in a professional scientific magazine detailing a new piece of research would be considered reliable. However, a personal blog or wiki site may not be. Never assume that what you read has been fact-checked, especially if it's a personal blog post or web article. Where possible, it's worth finding two or three sources for a fact before including it in your movie.

INTERVIEWS

These are usually with people who are relevant to the story. They could be witnesses to an event or experts on the subject you're covering. If you're planning to interview people, find out as much as you can about the people beforehand. This helps you to prepare meaningful and appropriate questions you can ask during the interview.

If you're planning to make a documentary, you need to find out as much as you can about your subject matter. Try starting your research by reading books or searching the Internet.

Finding the right balance

Your documentary might be about a subject close to your heart or something that you feel passionate about. Even so, the best documentaries offer balanced viewpoints. That means selecting facts that show both sides of the story, as well as interviewees with differing opinions. You can always conclude by agreeing with one side of the argument, but overall your movie should be even-handed.

Success Story

Trace Gaynor (right) and Stephen Sotor were just 11 years old when they made their first documentary movie. Their 2004 movie *Tween's Life* featured interviews with their friends. Two years later, their second movie, *Genie in a Bottle: Unleashed*, was shown at movie festivals around the world.

Writing a script

Whether you plan to tell a true story or one you've made up, you'll need to write a script. If you are making fiction, this contains the words you'd like your characters to say. If you're making a documentary, a script will contain what will be said between interview clips. For both types of movie, there will be lots of other important information. The following script excerpt contains some examples of what is in a script.

A script is an important document containing instructions. Scripts should include information about the location of the scene, the time of day, the words you'd like the actors to say, and movements you'd like them to make.

SCENE 1

TOM'S BEDROOM: DAY

TOM and JULIE stand by the window. TOM looks sad.

TOM

(Sighing)

I'm not sure this rain will ever end.

JULIE

The storm will pass eventually.

JULIE turns toward TOM.

What are you really thinking about?

TOM looks at JULIE, then down at the floor.

TOM

I guess I just miss Rex. He always loved playing in the rain.

JULIE hugs TOM.

JULIE

Do you remember that time he chased his own tail for half an hour?

TOM

(Smiling)

Yeah, that was funny. He was a great dog, but really stupid!

Cast and crew

Visit any major movie set and you'll see dozens of people buzzing around. Each person has a part to play in the production process. Some of the more common roles in movie and TV production include:

DIRECTOR
This person calls the shots by giving instructions to actors and camera operators.

PRODUCER
This person oversees the running of the entire project, leaving the director to concentrate on filming.

CINEMATOGRAPHER
He or she controls the style and look of the movie, usually by changing the lighting or by picking different types of camera lenses to use. This person works closely with a lighting crew.

CAMERA OPERATORS
They film the action. Many movies and TV shows have lots of cameras and operators to film scenes from different angles.

SOUND RECORDISTS
These people get sound recordings of the actors during filming. They may work with teams of technicians.

MAKEUP ARTIST
This person makes sure the actors and extras look like the characters they're portraying on-screen.

ACTORS (THE CAST)
These are people who play the characters you have created.

EXTRAS
Sometimes called "background actors," these people don't speak and are there to supplement the main characters—for example, in crowd scenes.

A director is at work.

This makeup artist is helping someone to get into character.

A little help from your friends

Try getting your classmates involved in your movie. They might have some great ideas, a burning desire to act, or even want to lend a hand with making costumes! If you're making a documentary, they could help with research, find people to interview, or even operate the camera.

STAY SAFE

When using the Internet, always get a parent, teacher, or other responsible adult to help you out. Remember not to talk to strangers through chat services, no matter how friendly they may seem.

Once you've found people for your movie's cast and crew, you need to think about filming locations. Your school may let you use the building for filming after hours or on weekends.

Location, location, location

So, where are you going to film your first masterpiece? You may need to find several different locations, depending on what your movie or TV show is about. You'll need places to set a fictional story or to film footage for a documentary.

Pro Tip

If the making of your movie or show involves filming members of the public, you need to get permission. This is known in the world of TV and movies as consent. You'll need to ask anyone being filmed, and those who own the locations you use, to sign a consent form. You can find templates for these consent forms online, but run these by an adult before you get them signed.

Get thinking!

You may need to be imaginative with your choices for filming locations. For example, it may be possible to film at school as long as you get permission. Also, local places of worship and community centers often have rooms you can rent for a small fee. Parks, friends' homes, sports fields, and the street where you live can also be useful free locations.

Your own home might seem like a boring choice, but with a bit of effort you can change its appearance to fit the movie. You could move furniture around, put up pictures or posters, or even use props. Objects such as drinking glasses, walking sticks, pens, bottles, and books can help your sets look real.

It's important that the costumes you choose reflect what's happening in the movie. For example, If the story is supposed to take place in winter, it would be inappropriate for an actress to be wearing a summer vacation outfit like the one below!

Preparing to shoot

If everything has gone according to plan, you should almost be ready to start filming, or shooting. Before you start, there are still a couple of pieces of the filmmaking jigsaw puzzle missing.

Shot list

A shot list is a scene-by-scene breakdown, in the form of a list, of everything a director wants to film. The shot list can be used to keep track of what a director needs to film as he or she moves along, even when making a documentary.

Unusual camera movements and shots make your project interesting. You don't need expensive equipment. Try mounting your camera on a skateboard for a moving shot. Or how about seeing the inside of a drawer as a character opens it? The shot list for the beginning of a scene may start as follows:

1. A shot to show the location and situation. This is called an establishing shot.
2. A long shot showing the main character in the distance.
3. A tracking shot following that character walking through a scene.
4. A medium shot of two characters meeting, possibly from the waist up.
5. A close-up of the two characters talking.

Storyboard

A storyboard is a step-by-step guide to how you want each scene to look. It looks a little like a comic strip. It can be used to help decide the kind of shots and camera angles you'd like to use in each scene.

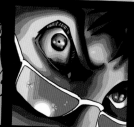

In animation, animators often follow a storyboard (like this one) and a shot list combined. This helps them to explain what they need to animate in great detail.

Getting your hands on hardware

The final step of the planning process is an important one: getting hold of filming equipment. There are a number of options, each with their own advantages and disadvantages. If you are having trouble finding any of it, research to see if there are filmmaking groups for young people in your area that can lend you their equipment.

Pro Tip

Smartphone

ADVANTAGES
- Easy to use
- Excellent for filming quickly

DISADVANTAGES
- Can only store small amounts of footage
- Poor picture quality
- Hard to hold still

Tablet computer

ADVANTAGES
- Excellent for filming quickly
- Large screen to play back footage

DISADVANTAGES
- Can only store small amounts of footage
- Poor picture quality

Webcam

ADVANTAGES
- Stores movie footage on a computer

DISADVANTAGES
- Needs to be connected to a computer
- Poor picture quality

Video camera/Camcorder

ADVANTAGES
- Great picture quality
- Designed for filmmaking
- More features that can be used during filming

DISADVANTAGES
- Can be expensive to buy

CHAPTER 3

Filming Your
MOVIE or TV SHOW

You are now ready to make movies! Remember that filming can be time-consuming and stressful, but it will all be worth it when you see the finished results!

After all that planning, you should now be ready to go. On the first day of filming, you're likely to experience a mixture of feelings—excitement, nervousness, and even a little stress as you remember all the things you need to do. This is natural. Just take your time and try to enjoy it.

No need to rush

Making movies and TV shows is a time-consuming process, so you'll need to be patient. Allow enough time for everything, since things can go wrong. For example, actors might forget their lines, or you may want to film a number of different versions of the same scene (known as takes) to try different things out.

It might also be tricky to get the answers you're looking for from interviewees, or something might go wrong with the equipment. You also need to allow time for people to change costumes, move between locations, and set up equipment. Filming a scene may only take a few minutes, but setting up the next scene might take three or four times as long!

Last-minute checks

Before you head to the set, or shoot, why not make a checklist to make sure you're fully prepared? The following list might be a good start:

- Copies of the script for every member of the cast and crew
- Shot list
- Camcorder/smartphone/tablet/webcam/microphones and other filming equipment
- Consent forms
- Addresses of filming locations
- Names of actors or interviewees
- Costumes and props

Lights, camera, action!

Depending on the type of movie or show you're filming, there are different ways to conduct a shoot. It's worth familiarizing yourself with the process before you start, especially if you have not done it before. There are no rules, though—if you have ideas you'd like to try out, just go for it!

Filming fiction

Traditionally, works of fiction are filmed by following the script, storyboard, and shot list. That means filming a number of takes of the same scene, often from different angles, until you're happy with the results. Once you've done that, you can move on to the next scene. Don't worry about recording more footage than you need—you can select the best parts to use later.

Don't just rely on the script to tell a story. You could use a montage that shows the passing of time. For example, if you are shooting a runner training for a race, you could use a mix of shots over several days set to background music. Also, don't forget continuity. This means making sure everything on the camera looks the same from shot to shot, from hairstyles to lighting.

If you're filming interviews, listen to the interviewees' answers. Don't be afraid to ask questions based on what they say, in addition to those you've prepared beforehand.

Filming footage of athletes in action from different angles could help make your sports documentary sparkle. You could even get the athletes themselves to talk over the action afterward. This is known in the business as a "voiceover."

Factual filming

The process for filming documentaries does not always follow a specific order. You can film the elements needed in any order you wish, recording interviews and additional footage as you go along. For example, if the documentary is about sports, you may want to film athletes training or competing. Also, if you find out something unexpected on the way, you may want to go back and interview somebody again. This additional footage is important, as it helps make the documentary interesting. You can edit it all in order later.

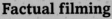

THE KNOWLEDGE

While some movies (and some TV shows) are still shot on photographic film, much recording is now done digitally. This means filming something on a digital camera, camcorder, smartphone, or tablet. Here, the recording is saved inside the device as computer data. The storage capacity of devices varies, so you may have to stop recording and transfer data to a computer or hard drive if you run out of space.

CHAPTER 4

Finishing Your TV MOVIE or SHOW

Finished movies are the result of a long period after shooting has finished, known as post-production. This part of filmmaking can sometimes take longer than the filming. During post-production, you have to select and sequence (known as editing) the best footage and then add any extra touches, such as music and special effects.

Following filming, the time-consuming task of editing begins. This is the process of turning the raw footage you've filmed into a masterpiece!

THE KNOWLEDGE

In the movie and TV production industry, a person responsible for editing is known as an editor. He or she is a trained specialist with a talent for selecting and joining together the best pieces of footage, usually under the supervision of the director.

Rough cut

The editing process can be quite time-consuming, as it involves digging through a lot of raw footage. It can take a skilled editor around three months to produce the first edit of a professional feature movie, known as the rough cut. Finishing the final cut might take another month.

The terms "rough cut" and "final cut" refer to the traditional process of physically cutting up and ordering photographic film. Today, most editing is done on computers, using special editing software.

Pro Tip

Editing software is available for smartphones and tablets, but most film editing is done on laptops or desktop computers. To use this method, you'll need to transfer the footage from the camera, phone, or tablet to a computer. This is normally very simple to do. It involves connecting the camera to the computer using a USB cord, then dragging the movie files to your computer's hard drive.

Final cut

To edit your movie, you'll need editing software. Luckily, there are lots of free programs out there. Most PCs now come with Windows Movie Maker installed. If not, it can be downloaded from the Microsoft web site for free. Some Apple devices come bundled with iMovie, which can also be bought cheaply from the App Store. If these don't suit your needs, there are plenty of other free editing software packages available. If it's not your personal computer, remember to ask permission before downloading software.

Useful tools

Every editing program is slightly different, but they all offer similar features. They all allow you to load film footage, select the parts you want to use, and then arrange them on-screen using a drag-and-drop system. You can shorten longer footage, stitch together different takes, and add effects.

Pro Tip

If you want to finish your movie quickly, there are smartphone apps and web sites that will help by doing it for you. A good example is Magisto, which edits together cool-looking videos using clips you've selected. While great for making movies quickly, these apps don't give you much control over the editing process.

If you know someone with experience editing film clips, why not get him or her to help you create your "final cut"? You can still call the shots, just like a professional movie director!

Editing software for beginners

Menu
This is where you'll find all the key controls for editing your movie, such as copy, cut, and paste, plus other useful tools.

Contents
Drag movie clips you'd like to use here, before putting them into your movie timeline.

FILE   EDIT   VIEW

Import

Export

Edit

Video 1

Timeline
This is where you arrange the clips that will make up your movie. There is sometimes a clock here, too, so you can see how long your movie is.

Preview window
Watch individual clips or the entire contents of the timeline.

Finishing touches

By now, you might have a rough cut of your movie that you're happy with. If so, you might want to add a few extra touches to make it stand out. Many free or inexpensive editing software packages include special visual effects that can be used to spice up your movie. Some programs also let you slow down or speed up footage, turn color images into black-and-white images, or completely change the soundtrack.

Sounds alive

Adding music or sound effects is a great way to make your movie even more memorable. For example, if you have made a movie about ghosts, you could:
- use spooky theme music to set the scene and create a chilling mood
- add sound effects, such as doors creaking, to make certain moments of the movie extra scary
- emphasize a big moment in the movie by adding music that enhances what you're seeing on-screen.

You can record voiceovers for documentaries and news reports using a microphone, computer, and voice recording software. This recording can then be dubbed onto the movie during the editing process.

Foley artists make sound effects for movies, often out of everyday objects. You could clap coconuts together to copy the sound of horses' hooves, or sprinkle rice onto a metal surface to create a sound like rain.

Most music is copyright-protected, meaning you can't use it in movies or TV shows without permission from the person who made it. Luckily, royalty-free music, which can be used without permission, also exists. You'll find this in online music libraries such as Freeplay Music and the YouTube Audio Library.

CHAPTER 5

Promoting Your
MOVIE or TV SHOW

One day, posters for your movies might be plastered at a movie theater. For now, you may have to settle for hanging up homemade posters at school.

Once you've put the finishing touches on your first movie or TV show, it's time to tell people about it. If you want people to see it, you'll need to turn it into a single video clip and save it, using a process called exporting. All editing software will let you export video. Then you'll need to develop a plan for showing people your work.

Promotion commotion

The process of raising awareness about a product or service is called marketing. Today, the success or failure of a movie or TV series can come down to how well it is marketed to the public. According to a 2014 report in *Hollywood Reporter*, the average worldwide marketing spend on a big-budget movie is a staggering $200 million. Much of this money is spent on posters and other advertisements on radio, television, and the Internet.

Get burning!

Clearly, you can't afford to spend much money on marketing your movie, but there are lots of less expensive things you can do. Why not burn some DVDs for those who helped you make the movie? It's good to get their feedback before you go public with the movie.

Many laptops and desktop computers have the ability to "burn" DVDs. If yours does, you'll need to get hold of some DVD-R discs.

Pro Tip

Most filmmakers try to raise interest in their movies by making trailers. These are short advertisements featuring action from the movie, with music and a voiceover explaining what the movie is all about. Try to make your own trailer for your movie.

In the showbiz industry, it's traditional to launch a new movie by holding a glitzy premiere.

This is a test

Before a movie's star-studded premiere, it will have already been shown to small groups of people at events called test screenings. During these screenings, people working in the movie industry or members of the public are asked to watch a movie. They give feedback on the movie by filling in a special questionnaire. These answers are mainly used to figure out how to market a movie, but sometimes they're even used to change the movie. Some big-budget movies can need reshoots.

The big premiere

When you're ready to launch your first big- or small-screen masterpiece, you could hold your own premiere. Invite your friends, family, and those who've helped you out to a special screening at home, school, or a local community center. You could even have a question-and-answer session at the end, where you talk about the making of the movie.

Make your own movie questionnaire

Try to hold your own test screening for friends, complete with questionnaires based on those used by movie studios! Here are a few questions to get you going, but feel free to think of your own:

What did you think of the movie overall?

Which characters/scenes did you like/dislike the most?

Would you recommend this movie to your friends?

What could we do to improve the movie?

What did you think of the ending?

If your movie or TV show gets an excited response, you know you're on the right track! If not, ask those who've seen it to provide detailed, honest feedback about where and how you could improve it.

Today, more people than ever before watch movies and TV shows online.

Sharing it with the world

The Internet is great for budding filmmakers. It allows them to get their work into the public domain without the need to rely on expensive marketing tricks, such as advertising campaigns. You could upload your movie or TV show to video-sharing sites such as YouTube and Vimeo. Remember, though, if you're under 13 years of age, get a responsible adult to do it for you.

The hard sell

Thousands of video clips are uploaded to sharing sites every minute, so you'll still have to work hard on promotion if you want your project to go viral. This is an expression used when something spreads quickly on the Internet. Getting a video to go viral is no easy task, but the following will give you a much greater chance of success:

- Keep your video clip short.
- Inspire your audience—for example, with amazing real-life stories.
- Be upbeat, funny, or include content likely to stir emotions.
- Link your video clip to current events or subjects that people are talking about online.

Success Story

Another great way to spread the word is to create your own YouTube channel. This allows you to post a number of video clips to one page, which viewers can subscribe to. This is what filmmaker Ari Gold did to promote his 2008 movie *Adventures of Power*. He posted more than 70 video clips to his channel, including footage not shown in the movie. His channel received more than 200,000 views and around 1,000 subscribers, and it increased sales of his DVDs.

Although he won a Student Oscar for his short movie *Helicopter*, Ari Gold still found it hard to raise interest in his feature-length comedy movie *Adventures of Power*. For this reason, he turned to YouTube to help spread the word.

Just the Beginning!

How have you found your filmmaking adventure? If all has gone according to plan, your head should already be full of ideas. You might be thinking about things you can do to promote your project and other movies and shows you can make in the future.

Once you have the filmmaking bug, you'll be hooked for life. Many movie directors began by making home movies during their teenage years.

Success Story

Steven Spielberg, one of the most successful directors of all time, began by making home movies as a teenager. He quickly found work in the industry, directing his first TV movie at the age of 24. He was only 28 when the movie *Jaws* was released, one of the biggest blockbusters of all time!

There's no limit!

The great thing about filmmaking is that the only limit is your imagination. The world is full of interesting subjects to investigate, stories to tell, and events to film. Every time you set out to make a new movie or TV show, the process will be a little bit easier. There will be gradual improvements in your scriptwriting, directing, filming, and editing skills.

You'll soon be finding all sorts of excuses to pursue your hobby. For example, if you have a school history project to do, you could film a re-creation of the events being discussed in class. You could make a video explaining how DNA works for a science project.

Career move

There is no limit to what you can do with filmmaking. If you're lucky, it could even lead to a career in the movie and TV industry. You might not be the director of a big-budget Hollywood smash hit yet, but you can still wow people with well-crafted documentaries, comedy sketch shows, or homemade TV dramas. Think big! And good luck!

Glossary

blockbuster hugely successful and popular movie, often one that also costs a lot of money to make

campaign planned sequence of events used to achieve a goal—for example, raising awareness of the release of a new movie through advertising and marketing

contemporary something happening right now, in the present time

continuity process of ensuring everything appearing "on camera" looks the same from shot to shot, from hairstyles to lighting

dubbing process of adding sounds (music, speaking, or effects) to a movie or television show

film noir style of crime movie renowned for the use of shady characters and minimal use of lighting. *Noir* means "black" in French.

Foley artist person who specializes in making and recording special effects for movies and TV shows

gangster movie type of crime movie that focuses on criminal gangs and their activities

genre style or category of movie—for example, thriller, comedy, or documentary

home movie movie made for personal use without special equipment—for example, a movie of a person's vacation

interviewee person who is being interviewed by someone

marketing process of raising awareness of a product or service in order to attract more customers or viewers

montage series of shots to show something happening over time

premiere first time a movie or television program is shown, either to the public or an invited audience of special guests

prop object the actors use on camera, in a movie or TV program

public domain content that is available to the public to legally use for free

reshoot when a cast and crew go back and film scenes, or parts of scenes, again after they think they have finished filming everything. This is usually based on feedback from a test screening.

romantic comedy (rom-com) style of funny movie based on love and relationships

set up arrange the position of cameras, scenery, and other equipment on a movie or TV shoot

soundtrack sound that accompanies the pictures on a movie or TV show, which can include speech, music, and effects

sub-genre small category of movie within a larger category. For example, a gangster movie would be in the larger category of crime movies.

test screening when members of the public and the movie industry are invited to watch and comment on a movie. Their comments can cause a movie to have reshoots or re-editing.

thriller type of movie or TV series known for being particularly exciting or gripping

voiceover voice in a movie or television show, of a person who is heard but not seen, or not seen talking

Find Out More

Books

Blofield, Robert. *How to Make a Movie in 10 Easy Lessons* (Super Skills).
   Irvine, Calif.: Walter Foster Jr., 2014.
Frost, Shelley. *Kids Guide to Movie Making*. Createspace, 2011.
Garza, Sarah. *Action!: Making Movies* (Time for Kids Nonfiction Readers).
   Huntington Beach, Calif.: Teacher Created Materials, 2013.
Jenks, Andrew. *Andrew Jenks: My Adventures as a Young Filmmaker*. New York:
   Scholastic, 2013.

Web sites

Coolspotters: The Mega Movie Making Guide for Kids
www.coolspotters.com/articles/the-mega-movie-making-guide-for-kids
This web site contains links to lots of great filmmaking resources for young
people. Here you can find information on putting together your first storyboard,
as well as tips on shooting and editing your first movie.

Media Match Magazine: TV and Movie Job Descriptions
www.media-match.com/usa/media/jobtypes/job-descriptions.php
If you're interested in working in movies or TV one day, this web site has lots
of great information about different jobs. For example, there is information on
well-known roles, such as actor and director. The web site also includes details
of lesser-known specialized jobs, such as aerial specialist, costume designer,
and Foley artist.

No Film School
www.nofilmschool.com
This is an excellent web site for would-be filmmakers. It is designed to help
fans of movies and TV production learn from one another. Expect step-by-step
videos, industry insights, and advice on equipment.

Further research

The good news is that, these days, you can find lots of useful information for budding filmmakers on the Internet. There are lots of tutorials on YouTube, and even groups for budding directors on social networks such as Facebook.

Would you like to be taught the basics of filmmaking by professionals? If so, there are lots of companies and organizations that offer visits and classes for schoolchildren. There may also be a free filmmaking group in your area, where you can exchange ideas, borrow equipment, and learn from like-minded people. If you're going to join a group, take a responsible adult along with you.

If you're stuck thinking up ideas, get together with friends or classmates to put together a short movie or TV show for a school project. Alternatively, you could test out your skills by making a movie about a school club, group, or sports team. If your school has a drama group, you could offer to film its next production. Then, turn it into a DVD for members to keep.

If you need music for your movies and TV shows, speak to any musician friends. They might like to create the soundtrack for the piece you're working on. You could even make a music video for the school band or any friends who have started their own group.

Index